GOD'S LOVE FOR US

Retold A-Z: Book 1

AUTHOR: KIMBERLY JOY CARTER

ILLUSTRATOR: VLADIMIR CEBU

ISBN-13: 978-0-578-43859-7

Dedication

This book is dedicated to my Lord and Savior, Jesus Christ, who has remained faithful to loving me, even in my sin.

To my children, Kaden and Taliah. God's greatest gift has been motherhood. The Lord has always seen us through, and because of Christ, we always win.

A is for Adam.

Whom God created first,
Gave power to rule,
Name all living things,
And dominion in the earth.

B is for Blessed.

God blessed Adam with a wife.

From Adam's rib, Created Eve

And breathed into her, life.

God did not think it best

For Adam to be alone

So He blessed him with a helpmeet

For him to call his own.

C is for Command.

God commanded Adam, "eat of every tree freely."

Except from the Tree of Good and Evil

It will lead to death, believe me.

D is for Deceiver.

Like the Big Bad Wolf, people sometimes pull you in with lies.

Then all of a sudden, you're doing what you know to be wrong,

Similar to Eve, you listened, knowing it wasn't right.

E is for Eve.

Who entertained the Serpent.

"Are you kidding me? Just take a bite.

Trust me, it will all be worth it.

You'll be equal to the Lord.

Have knowledge of good and evil.

I wonder if Eve was fully aware

Such power would be lethal.

F is for The Fall.

Eve fell by taking a bite of the fruit.

She convinced Adam too.

God came looking for them throughout the garden,

But they hid. They didn't know what to do.

Isn't it funny how we run away or try to cover sins?

When it's always more righteous and honorable

to admit what we did.

G is for Grace.

Since they disobeyed;

1. Men must work to eat.

2. Women have babies in pain.

3. The serpent must crawl on its belly.

4. In the garden, Adam and Eve no longer remained.

The punishment could have been much worse.

But this is what we call GRACE.

When God doesn't give us what we deserve

But another chance to do things the righteous way.

H is for the Human Race.

Which all started with Adam and Eve.
Eve gave birth to Cain and Abel,
These were the sons she conceived.
Cain was the oldest, Abel was the younger son,
Even though both mom and dad were present
Brotherly love....There seemed to be none.

I is for Issues.

I is for the issues

These two brothers were at odds.

Cain was jealous of his brother because God was more

pleased with Abel's offerings from his First Flocks.

Cain must've thought to himself, "God, I gave you an

offering of fruit. But clearly, you like Abel better

when I

want to be important too."

J is for Jealousy.

Jealousy ate away at Cain

Leading him to hate when he should love

He invited Abel to the fields

Only to slay him

Would you call this brotherly love?

Why did he hold the anger in? Why didn't Cain tell God

what he feels?

From this, we can all learn the lesson, that at our

worst

with God, it's best to keep it real.

K is for All-Knowing.

This means we serve a Super God.

He has the power to know everything.

No man or thing can compare to Him.

No Spiderman, Batman, or Marvel Team.

God knew Cain didn't offer Him the best.

With God, we can't pretend.

From Adam and Eve, we learn we can't hide.

Just obey, we'll be better off in the end.

L is for Listen

Listen to the Lord's commands.

Be doers of His word.

Offer God the first, your best

Ask yourself "What is this worth?"

If you find envy in your heart, ask the Lord to

remove.

Love what is unique about you from others and know

that

there is something special inside you.

M is for Multiply.

The people began to multiply and disobeyed God's will.

Watching such bad behavior eventually led God to want to kill.

Kill the evil he watched take place on earth, and start all over again.

Recreate a brand-new people who would love and serve only Him.

Though many were evil, there was one he'd spare, the entire family he would save.

A blameless man, known as righteous, and Noah was his name.

N is for Noah.

Noah was a worshiper, who desired to please God.

When the flood came, God would save Him because

Noah

was on God's squad.

He gave him the command to build a giant boat that

would keep him safe.

The boat was large, with three levels, to save Noah's

family while displaced.

O is for Obey.

He took one female and male of every animal because all

others would be dead.

His wife, sons, and their wives joined him for the long

journey ahead.

It rained 40 days and 40 nights, but Noah and his

family remained dry.

The amazing love of God our Father, they were able

to rest and abide.

P is for Peace.

Peace is what God gave them,

Even though for days it rained.

It took 150 days for the waters to recede (dry up)

But in God's care, they all remained.

Q is for Quiet.

While waiting for the water to dry up

God no longer spoke.

Can you imagine what Noah may have thought? Where is

God? How long will we be on this boat?

But God was QUIET during the process. He already gave

Noah the directions he would need.

Sometimes it's just a matter of waiting, standing still, and

obeying, so take heed.

R is for Raven.

Noah sent a Raven that flew high, to and fro

Hoping it would give a sign if the land was dry enough

for

them to go

Then he sent a dove out, for the next couple of

weeks

First, it came back with nothing.

But the second time, returned with an olive leaf.

The third time symbolized everything was dry

For the dove never returned.

The number 3, a sign of God's Rule

His Sovereignty was learned.

S is for Sacrifice.

Once the land had dried

Off the ark, Noah, his family, and animals went.

God told him that all must exit the boat

He built an altar and SACRIFICED to show what God

meant.

Not only did God spare Noah's life, family, and promise

Never to destroy all mankind.

But God told Noah, be fruitful and multiply, for my

promise,

a rainbow will be a sign.

T is for Tower of Babel.

One day, the people had an idea to build a tower so high.

Like a stairway going to heaven, a tower reaching the sky.

It's called a ziggurat.

It wasn't like the buildings we now see.

Except the tower wasn't built for God.

Let's learn why this building displeased Thee.

U is for Unity.

In Unity, the people built this tower

In one language, they all agreed

They wanted to make a name for themselves

To be held in high esteem.

Unity can be a powerful force

We must think about how it can be used.

For bullying, teasing, and mistreating others

Or volunteering, serving, and showing love to other

youth.

V is for Vice.

To God, the people's reason to build was vice,

Evil, and against His will

No people or things should be respected so high

At His name, all things should keep still

So God decided to confuse their language

They were unable to talk and agree

No longer working in unity

But divided, they moved about. He scattered thee.

W is for Worship.

It's why we were created.

It's not about what we sing or if we cry.

We worship in our living

Keeping God our center

The Master and Ruler of our lives.

We show what God is worth

in our obedience to Him, our giving, and how we treat

each other is true worship unto Him.

X is for Examine.

Let us learn to eXamine what we do
but more importantly, why we do it
Ask ourselves, will this be pleasing to God?
We must question, then why would we do it?
How does it bring Him honor?
Does it display His love?
Will it point others to believe in His power
and accept His unfailing love?

Y is for You.

You are fearfully and wonderfully made.

Understand that's why God never gave up on you.

He knew there would never be enough sacrifices to

forgive

our sins, and sent Jesus to die for you too.

Jesus Christ is called the 2nd Adam because as we

learned, the 1st one made some mistakes.

But this new Adam, who we call Jesus, came in the

form

of man, perfect, but took our place.

Z is for Zeal.

It's with zeal I share these truths with you

Of Adam, Eve, Cain, Abel, Noah, and the Tower of

Babel

too.

That points us to the Good News of Jesus Christ, the

Son

of God, who died and rose for you!

NOTES

Adam and Eve	Genesis 2:4-3:24
Cain and Abel	Genesis 4:1-16
Noah's Ark	Genesis 7 - 10
The Tower of Babel	Genesis 11

Alphabetical Index